D0064996

NUDE DESCENDING A STAIRCASE

POEMS | SONGS | A BALLAD

NUDE DESCENDING
A STAIRCASE

BY X. J. KENNEDY

DOUBLEDAY & COMPANY, INC.
Garden City, New York ` 1961

Some of the poems in this book were first printed in *Arbor*, *The Beloit Poetry Journal*, *Epoch*, *Generation*, *Hudson Review*, *Inland*, *The New Yorker*, *Paris Review* and *Poetry* in America; in *The Cornhill Magazine* in England; and appeared in the anthologies *Best Poems of 1958* (Pacific Books, Inc.) and *Literary Types and Themes* (Holt, Rinehart & Winston). The poems "Epitaph for a Postal Clerk," "On a Child Who Lived One Minute" and "Little Elegy" appeared originally in *The New Yorker*. An earlier version of the poem "All-Knowing Rabbit" appeared in *Spearhead*, edited by Thomas Henry Carter.

For MY FATHER AND MOTHER

AUTHOR'S NOTE

When you offer a first book of verse, it may be presumptuous to admit your debts to people. Still, I am unable to let these poems stand without trying to pay thanks to certain young poets of Ann Arbor with whom I have exchanged criticism, among them Keith Waldrop, James Camp, Donald Hope and Dallas Wiebe (the word *cockcrow* in the poem "At the Ghostwriter's Deathbed" is his); to Arno Bader of the University of Michigan for his instruction, so helpful especially to the poem "The Sirens"; to Donald Hall, John Frederick Nims and other editors who chided me into working harder; to Claire McAllister for making me aware of the tune that "In a Prominent Bar in Secaucus One Day" may be sung to; and not least to Naomi Burton, whose trust in my work reminded me that despair is a sin, and who encouraged me to put this book together.

Ann Arbor, Michigan
April, 1961

CONTENTS

ONE

TWO: SONGS & A BALLAD

INTERMISSION WITH PEANUTS

THREE

ONE |

FIRST CONFESSION

Blood thudded in my ears. I scuffed,
   Steps stubborn, to the telltale booth
Beyond whose curtained portal coughed
   The robed repositor of truth.

The slat shot back. The universe
   Bowed down his cratered dome to hear
Enumerated my each curse,
   The sip snitched from my old man's beer,

My sloth pride envy lechery,
   The dime held back from Peter's Pence
With which I'd bribed my girl to pee
   That I might spy her instruments.

Hovering scale-pans when I'd done
   Settled their balance slow as silt
While in the restless dark I burned
   Bright as a brimstone in my guilt

Until as one feeds birds he doled
   Seven Our Fathers and a Hail
Which I to double-scrub my soul
   Intoned twice at the altar rail

Where Sunday in seraphic light
   I knelt, as full of grace as most,
And stuck my tongue out at the priest:
   A fresh roost for the Holy Ghost.

ON A CHILD WHO
LIVED ONE MINUTE

Into a world where children shriek like suns
Sundered from other suns on their arrival,
She stared, and saw the waiting shape of evil,
But couldn't take its meaning in at once,
So fresh her understanding, and so fragile.

Her first breath drew a fragrance from the air
And put it back. However hard her agile
Heart danced, however full the surgeon's satchel
Of healing stuff, a blackness tiptoed in her
And snuffed the only candle of her castle.

O let us do away with elegiac
Drivel! Who can restore a thing so brittle,
So new in any jingle? Still I marvel
That, making light of mountainloads of logic,
So much could stay a moment in so little.

AT THE STOPLIGHT
BY THE PAUPERS' GRAVES

Earth has been saved them but they won't give in,
Won't lie down quiet, as they did before,
Though all is as it was: two children
To a bed, and the rat-wind scudding at the door.

Skull against skull, they won't stretch out at ease
Their jammed arms, won't set grass to root for good.
Perennials that came up only once
Struggle and dry down from their stones of wood.

My engine shudders as if about to stall
But I've no heart to wait with them all night.
That would be long to tense here for a leap,
Thrall to the remote decisions of the light.

FACES FROM A BESTIARY

Suggested by the twelfth century
Livre des Créatures *of Philip de Thaun*

I

The Lion sleeps with open eyes
That none may take him by surprise.
The Son of God he signifies

For when a Lion stillborn lies
His mother circles him and cries.
Then on the third day he will rise.

II

Hyena is a beast to hate.
No man hath seen him copulate.
He is unto himself a mate.

You who this creature emulate
Who with your mirrors fornicate
Do not repent. It is too late.

LANDSCAPES WITH SET-SCREWS

I

THE AUTUMN IN NORFOLK SHIPYARD

Is a secret one infers
From camouflage. Scrap steel
Betrays no color of season,
Corrosion works year-round.
But in sandblasted stubble
Lurks change: parched thistle burr,
Blown milkweed hull—dried potholes
After tides reassume their foam.

Destroyers mast to mast,
Mechanical conifers,
Bear pointed lights. Moored tankers
Redden slow as leaves.
Under the power crane
Dropped girders lie like twigs,
In drydock ripened tugs
Burst pod-wide—ringbolts bobble
To quiet upon steel-plate
Mud. A flake of paint falls,

Green seas spill last year's needles.

AIRPORT IN THE GRASS

Grasshopper copters whir,
Blue blurs
Traverse dry air,

Cicadas beam a whine
On which to zero in flights
Of turbojet termites,

A red ant carts
From the fusilage of the wren that crashed
Usable parts

And edging the landingstrip,
Heavier than air the river
The river
The rustbucket river
Revs up her motors forever.

IN FAITH OF RISING

When all my dust lies strewn
Over the roundbrinked ramparts of the world,
I can be gathered, sinew and bone
Out of the past hurled
Delaylessly as I
Flick thoughts back that replace
Lash to dropped lid, lid to eye,
Eye to disbanded face.
No task to His strength, for He
Is my Head—Him I trust
To stray the presence of His mind to me
Then cast down again
Or recollect my dust.

TO BREAK A MARBLE BLOCK

Croon to the stone that draws
Your dense hand onward. Supplicate
Galatea that of her own choice
She let fall from her lines
Stone swaddles with bumbling clatter,
Into your arms glide forth,
Only a faint cloth of stone dust
Across concessive loins.

But let you once run hand
Across pores breathing in her cheek
And smile, and say, I made me this—
Then shall you rut in stone.
Shall stone give birth to stone
And stone swing cradled in stone arms,
To cold bald stone stone croon
And stone to ravenous stone give suck.

| INSCRIPTIONS AFTER FACT

for Frank Brownlow

I   DECLARE WAR AGAINST HEAVEN

Not in silk robes but the hard hides of bulls,
Tusk of the boar and the stiff quill of the swan
Gods garb them, tread our world. Run, woman, run
Lest trolled in bed you bear strange bellyfuls.

Truant from home stars and from right spouse,
A god by self conceived and of self born
Sets out for manhood, halts in the halfway house
Of beast. But it is man he caps with horn.

Between what stubs one's knuckle and what but seems,
Between goat-paddock and god-rampant heaven,
Must man contend two ravening extremes
For his own women?

Shall he not rage who, having tied a bib
Round a fair boy that he thinks of his own make,
Fed him his porridge, taught him patty-cake,
Finds a constrictor throttled in his crib?

What child under a rooftree can sleep safe
While skies uncoil and phalloi slither down?
Will woman, the onslaught of a swan once known,
Think man a goose and give him up for life?

Drive! drive them back! Breast them with bow-
Sprits taut, stand fast, O rout them back to Heaven!
Let not a man-jack among them batter through!
Then kneel once more, slay beasts to be forgiven.

Adam's first wife had soft lips but no soul:
He looked her in the eye, back looked a hole.
Her small ear lay, a dry well so profound
No word he pebbled in it drew a sound.

Could he complete what God had left half-wrought?
He practiced in a looking lake, he taught
Stray rudiments of wriggle, where to stand
Her liltless feet. She handed him her hand.

Her breasts stood up but in them seemed to rise
No need for man. He roamed lone in her thighs
And inmost touching, most knew solitude:
In vacant rooms, on whom can one intrude?

O let down mercy on a poor man who clings
To echoes, beds him with imaginings!
Sweet Lord, he prayed, *with what shade do I lie?*
Second came she whom he begot us by.

Stayed in one place and did no work
But warble ditties a bit loose,
Strike poses, primp, bedeck their rock
With primrose boxes. Odysseus

Salt-lipped, long bandied before winds,
Heard in his loins a bass chord stir,
Said to his men, 'Men, stop your ears—
I need not, being an officer.'

Under the deaf indifferent tread
Of wood on water, round each oar
Broke like the grapes of Ilium
Ripening clusters of blue air

And when those soft sounds stole, there grew
The notion as he champed his bit
That love was all there was, and death
Had something to be said for it.

Roared as the music sweetened, railed
Against his oarsmen's bent wet slopes,
Imprisoned in propriety
And pagan ethic. Also ropes.

Sails strummed. The keel drove tapestries
Of distance on the sea's silk-loom
Leaving those simple girls beyond
Woven undone rewoven foam

To wonder: had they lost their touch?
Unbroken yet, a woof of sea
Impelled him to his dying dog,
Pantoufles, and Penelope.

He touched her face and gooseflesh crept—
He loved her as it were
Not for her look though it was deep
But what he saw in her.

Drew her up wobbling in his arms,
Laid lips by her smooth cheek
And would have joined the two of him
In one cohesive Greek

When soft by his obdurate ear
Like lips, two ripples pursed—
These syllables distinct and pure
Bubbled to air, and burst:

'Oh keep your big feet to yourself
Good sir, goddammit stop!
I'm not that sort of pool at all!
I'll scream! I'll call a cop!

'Settle me back in my right bed
Or you shall edge your skiff
Through ice as limber as your eyes,
As blue, as frozen stiff.'

Athens, U. S. Sixth Fleet, March 1953

By the aisle on a stone bench
In the Theater of Dionysus
I make a flock of Greek kids smile
Sketching them Mickey Mouses

Where beery Aristophanes
By sanction till night's fall
Ribbed Eleusinian mysteries
With queer-joke and pratt-fall.

On high from the sacked Parthenon
A blackbird faintly warbles.
Sellers of paperweights resell
The Elgin marbles.

Here where queen-betrayed
Agamemnon had to don
Wine-purple robes, boys in torn drabs
Try my whitehat on,

Over stones where Orestes fled
The sonorous Furies
Girls hawking flyspecked postcards
Pursue the tourist.

Here in her anguish-mask
Andromache
Mourned her slain son—'Young man,
Aren't you from Schenectady?'

As I trudge down, a pebble breaks
Rattling across stone tiers,
Scattering echoes: do I kick
A watcher's skull downstairs?

Silence imponders back
As I take the stage, the pebble
Stilled on a lower tier.
Trailing home now, the child rabble.

I stand in the center of the stage,
Could speak, but the sun's setting
In back of neon signs. Night unsheathes
Her chill blade. Better be getting

Back to the destroyer, radared bark,
No thresh of oars, sails with gods' crests—
Does the wind stir through the dark
Or does a throng of ghosts?

I run. Inaudible laughter drives
Offstage my spirit
As in the parched grass, wind routs
A white shiver before it.

LITTLE ELEGY

for a child who skipped rope

Here lies resting, out of breath,
Out of turns, Elizabeth
Whose quicksilver toes not quite
Cleared the whirring edge of night.

Earth whose circles round us skim
Till they catch the lightest limb,
Shelter now Elizabeth
And for her sake trip up Death.

OVERHEARD IN THE LOUVRE

Said the Victory of Samothrace,
What winning's worth this loss of face?

TWO |

SONGS & A BALLAD

IN A PROMINENT BAR
IN SECAUCUS ONE DAY

*To the tune of "The Old Orange Flute" or
the tune of "Sweet Betsy from Pike"*

In a prominent bar in Secaucus one day
Rose a lady in skunk with a topheavy sway,
Raised a knobby red finger—all turned from their beer—
While with eyes bright as snowcrust she sang high and clear:

'Now who of you'd think from an eyeload of me
That I once was a lady as proud as could be?
Oh I'd never sit down by a tumbledown drunk
If it wasn't, my dears, for the high cost of junk.

'All the gents used to swear that the white of my calf
Beat the down of the swan by a length and a half.
In the kerchief of linen I caught to my nose
Ah, there never fell snot, but a little gold rose.

'I had seven gold teeth and a toothpick of gold,
My Virginia cheroot was a leaf of it rolled
And I'd light it each time with a thousand in cash—
Why the bums used to fight if I flicked them an ash

'Once the toast of the Biltmore, the belle of the Taft,
I would drink bottle beer at the Drake, never draft,
And dine at the Astor on Salisbury steak
With a clean tablecloth for each bite I did take.

'In a car like the Roxy I'd roll to the track,
A steel-guitar trio, a bar in the back,
And the wheels made no noise, they turned over so fast,
Still it took you ten minutes to see me go past.

'When the horses bowed down to me that I might choose,
I bet on them all, for I hated to lose.
Now I'm saddled each night for my butter and eggs
And the broken threads race down the backs of my legs.

'Let you hold in mind, girls, that your beauty must pass
Like a lovely white clover that rusts with its grass.
Keep your bottoms off barstools and marry you young
Or be left—an old barrel with many a bung.

'For when time takes you out for a spin in his car
You'll be hard-pressed to stop him from going too far
And be left by the roadside, for all your good deeds,
Two toadstools for tits and a face full of weeds.'

All the house raised a cheer, but the man at the bar
Made a phonecall and up pulled a red patrol car
And she blew us a kiss as they copped her away
From that prominent bar in Secaucus, N.J.

SEINE RIVER BLUES

Dreamed you were with me
Doing what you used to do.
Yes I dreamed you were with me
Doing what you used to do.
Woke up in the morning
With my pillow tore in two.

Looking in the looking-glass
To see who I could see.
Looking-glass man he holler,
Who that looking in at me?

Counting up my money,
Just the lightweight kind of francs.
A fairy said, I'll keep you
But I said no thanks.

Watching people from Decatur
In their silks and furs
Riding solidgold Rolls Royces
Saying HIS and HERS.

High up in my cherrytree
There's a blackbird sits
Eating messes off my cherries
Spitting down the pits.

Going over to the Right Bank,
Tell American Express
Send my letters to the river,
That's my permanent address.

Write me a letter baby
Where that black water slides.
Write me a letter baby.
Make your little bed inside.

BARKING DOG BLUES

I hear those barking dog blues
Every getting-out-of-bed of day.
I hear those barking dog blues
Every getting-out-of-bed of day,
Barking dog blues
That chase my other blues away.

Mister Municipal Dog-Catcher
Won't you throw me in your pound?
Cause I just might bite somebody
If you leave me running round.

Baby, some men want to marry—
Me, I'd rather go to jail.
You drive me round in circles
Like a tin can tied to my tail.

Quit your messing round my little dog
Cause my big dog got a bone.
If you don't want my big dog
Leave my little dog alone.

Hear me barking Monday morning
In the driving rain.
I'll lay down in your kennel
But I won't wear your chain.

THE MAN IN THE MANMADE MOON

A BALLAD

I

When the lean recruit threw a shaky salute
The Major lay down his *Life*
And he fingered Bill's file and flicked him a smile
As you'd open a switchblade knife,

Popped a cigarette case underneath Bill's face.
Bill accepted a butt and bit it
And the air went *baloom!*—into the room
A little gold jet flew, and lit it.

Then they both blew smoke till the silence broke:
'Airman Beale—oh no, let's not be formal—
My boy, you've scored straight across the board
Such an absolute norm you're abnormal.

'Oh we've mapped the terrain of your adequate brain,
Taken soundings with sonar beams.
A Congressional probe of your frontal lobe
Finds you natural in your dreams.

'You'd be fit, of course, for the ranks of the Force,
But we're racing the hand of extinction!
There's a mission, m' boy, that may better employ
A man of your lack of distinction.

'After months of strain our mechanical brain
Has computed a blunderproof plan
To persuade the race that there's nothing like space,
That a vacuum's good for a man.'

Bill Beale took a sip on his filtertip
And he said, 'Well I don't know as I
Care to gamble the skin I'll be standing up in
When I marry my Lizabeth Bligh.'

But the Major began to set forth his plan
Over eight or ten sociable sloe gins—
As they slumped to the floor, esprit de corps
Played the Greek horse to Bill Beale's Trojans.

II

On a dune of sand in that no man's land
Where the hydrogen bombs hold practise,
With nothing but Bill within range to kill
And a button of stunted cactus,

They stuck Bill Beale in a ball of steel
On the nose of a seven-stage rocket.
They packed a supply of ham-on-rye
And they put it into his pocket.

Just to polish and tune that little steel moon
They'd been to no end of bother.
They fed Bill a last quick-frozen repast
And they said him a fast Our Father.

And he lay, poor lad, on his launching pad
And the Major droned: 'Thirty-one—thirty—'
On the brink of the blast it struck him at last:
Was he doing his Lizabet dirty?

Then the rocket whoomed and the world's weight slammed
As an elephant tromps on a spider
And there in his hammock Bill observed his stomach
Growing wider and wider   and wider.

Through bulletproof glass Bill Beale saw pass
In a blur the ionosphere
Where the meteors flash as they twist to ash
And there's noplace to stop for beer.

Bill circled the earth for all he was worth.
Every time he traversed an ocean
They gave him a day of overseas pay
And the Major a whole promotion.

As he lay on his face in outer space
And snored off his mid-day meal,
Some razored a wrist while others kissed
By the light of the full Bill Beale.

Bill squinted below at the blue seas' flow
As the earth eased over on her side
So lazy and warm you could take your arm
And gather her close like a bride.

It put Bill in mind of his woman behind
And a hot tear scalded his eye—
'Let me out of here! Sweet Lord, I fear
I'll nevermore see Liz Bligh!'

Bill beat in a rage at his cast-steel cage
And he bellowed, 'Oh set me down!
I want to tread dirt till my bare feet hurt
And the soles of 'em both turn brown!

'Oh, what I needs is some worms and weeds
And a couple of clods to stand on!
I'll nevermore leave!'—but he didn't perceive
The meteor sneaking up behind him with great alacrity.

And way out there past the reach of air
Where there's nothing to be resisted
Where there's nothing at all but a slow free-fall
And the up and the down grow twisted

Where the sunspots seethe, where the vapors writhe
Round the lip of the red sun's crucible,
Where the meteor's heart forms an iron dart
As it burns to its irreducible,

To the vacuous sound of moons turning round
And round, times out of mind,
Billie Beale and his soul met the perfect hole
And the three of those things combined.

III

On a moonlit night while the hills lay white,
On a night of a crescent Bill,
When the larks in their nest slept breast to breast
And the Chevrolet cars lay still,

Liz lifted her stare through the quiet air
And she said, 'There my lover-man blazes!
I'll keep him my soul like a glowing coal
Though his own wanes dim by phases.'

One day Lizabet by her TV set
Sat a-twiddlin' the knobs and mopin'
When the news said: 'Flash!—you'll receive Bill's trash
In a pine box you'd better not open.'

Her face went white as fluorescent light
And the face in the screen grew unsteady.
As she shook in her shock, came a knuckledy knock
And a hoarse voice: 'Coffin, lady!'

As she Xed her sign on the dotted line
Poor Lizabet's mind grew murky.
All there was of Bill was a little black pill
F.O.B. Albuquerque.

Well, she rolled that pill up Capitol Hill
And she sang to both houses of Congress
In a voice that shook, with a lunatic look—
Oh she'd aged like an old whoremongress—

'Coal black is the raven, coal black is the rook,
Coal black is the shark in the billow.
Where I once had a Bill to drive back my chill
There's a cold blackeyed pea on my pillow.

'In my dreams once more I stood at his door
Crying, Love, let me in let me in
For the loud winds rave in my permanent wave
And the raindrops dilute my gin.

'And the door swung wide and there inside
At the height of the man I'd lost
Hung a featureless face full of outer space
On a neck like a jet exhaust.'

IV

They blew a slow taps over Bill Beale's corpse
That set poor Lizabet screechin'
And he went to his grave with a new flag to wave
From the local American Legion.

Liz lay with her head on his fresh-dug bed,
She lay there a long time calling.
When the steel-grey snow fell down to her brow
She just let the snow go on falling.

And there grew from the clay where the two of them lay
As the earth took its time to settle,
A sweet pea vine and a blackeyed pea vine
And a rose in a vacuum bottle.

The blackeyed pea and the blossoming pea,
They twined arms round each other.
The rust-red rose and the cold Thermos,
They thinned to air together.

INTERMISSION
WITH PEANUTS

FOR CHILDREN
IF THEY'LL TAKE THEM

I   THE MAN

The man
With the tan
Hands
Who stands
And scoops up
Hot
Roast
Chestnuts
In cups
Of old
News
Folded
Like perching
Birds

Sold us
A few
New
Words.

King Tut
Crossed over the Nile
On steppingstones of crocodile.

King Tut!
His mother said,
Come here this minute!
You'll get wet feet.
King Tut is dead

And now King Tut
Tight as a nut
Keeps his big fat Mummy shut.

King Tut,
        tut, tut.

LEWIS CARROLL

Click! down the black whiterabbithole
Of his light-tight box he swooped
Littlegirls (women in capsule form,
My dear the better to eat you).

On tiptoe past intimidated primroses,
His head ateeter on its collar wall,
The Reverend Mr Dodgson longdivided
God's cipher (1 goes 3 × into 3)

And shrinking as his Alice grew, rejected
The little flask of love that said *Drink Me*.

THE PHANTOM
OF WOODLAND HOMES

Steamshovel forceps creak,
Budge the entrenched stump—
Its gums smoothed, now the hill smiles
With artificial timber.
But even now some nights
When white TVs in phases gleam
From every sunken livingroom,
The final child bestowed to bed,
There comes a ghost with beaver teeth,
Gobbets of fungus-moss for hair
And hootowl holes instead of eyes,
Who drifts the snippered breezeways, steals
Through parked cars strewing porcupines
In glove compartment and back seat—
At dawn his hawk-clawed prints surround
Petunias stifled in their plots,
The tricycle found tied in knots.

THE AGED WINO'S COUNSEL
TO A YOUNG MAN ON
THE BRINK OF MARRIAGE

A two-quart virgin in my lap,
With hands that shook I peeled her cap
And filched a kiss. It warmed me so,
I raised my right hand, swore *I do*—
We merged our fleshes, I and she,
In mutual indignity.

Now, when I hear of wives that freeze,
Bitter of lip, with icebound knees,
Who play high-card for social bets
And lose, and feed you carp croquettes,
Who nap all day and yak all night
What Ruth told Min—now which was right?—
Who count with glee your falling hairs
But brood a week on one of theirs,
Who'll see your parkerhouse poke out
Before they'll take a stitch, who pout
At change of moon, as I hear tell,
I say: son, wed you half as well.

CARRYING ON WITHOUT HIM

As if the blows of ten-ton trucks
   Were what one took in stride,
Not even staggered in their tracks,
   His shoes with strings still tied

Stepped giant through a greenhouse pane
   As if they'd choose therein
Commemorations for the man
   Whose bearers they had been.

The florist goggled. Reined up short,
   The left shoe took its stand,
The right arced up: a pot of dirt
   Exploded in his hand.

Pedestrians two such as these,
   How could one grow to love?—
Pure shoes below the displaced knees,
   Dismounted air above.

Now who would think two leather graves,
   The clods we rise to don,
Could shrug us, no more be our slaves,
   And footloose carry on?

Absorbed, an empire leaps too late
   And while the brake still squeals
Some flunky trampled underfoot
   Is kicking up his heels.

EPITAPH FOR A POSTAL CLERK

Here lies wrapped up tight in sod
Henry Harkins c/o God.
On the day of Resurrection
May be opened for inspection.

ARS POETICA

The goose that laid the golden egg
Died looking up its crotch
To find out how its sphincter worked.

Would you lay well? Don't watch.

THREE |

B NEGATIVE

M / 60 / 5 FT 4 / W PROT

You know it's April by the falling-off
In coughdrop boxes—fewer people cough—
    By daisies' first white eyeballs in the grass
And every dawn more underthings cast off.

Though plumtrees stretch recovered boughs to us
And doubledecked in green, the downtown bus,
    Love in one season—so your stab-pole tells—
Beds down, and buds, and is deciduous.

Now set down burlap bag. In pigeon talk
The wobbling pigeon flutes on the sidewalk,
    Struts on the breeze and clicks leisurely wings
As if the corn he ate grew on a stalk.

So plump he topples where he tries to stand,
He pecks my shoelaces, come to demand
    Another sack, another fifteen cents,
And yet—who else will eat out of my hand?

It used to be that when I laid my head
And body with it down by you in bed
    You did not turn from me nor fall to sleep
But turn to fall between my arms instead

And now I lay bifocals down. My feet
Forget the twist that brought me to your street.
    I can't make out your face for steamed-up glass
Nor quite call back your outline on the sheet.

I know how, bent to a movie magazine,
The hobo's head lights up, and from its screen
    Imagined bosoms in slow motion bloom
And no director interrupts the scene:

I used to purchase in the Automat
A cup of soup and fan it with my hat
    Until a stern voice from the changebooth crashed
Like nickels: *Gentlemen do not do that.*

Spring has no household, no abiding heat,
Pokes forth no bud from branches of concrete,
    Nothing to touch you, nothing you can touch—
The snow, at least, keeps track of people's feet.

The springer spaniel and the buoyant hare
Seem half at home reclining in mid-air
    But Lord, the times I've leaped the way they do
And looked round for a foothold—in despair.

The subway a little cheaper than a room,
I browse the *News*—or so the guards assume—
    And there half-waking, tucked in funny sheets,
I hurtle within my mile-a-minute womb.

Down streets that wake up earlier than wheels
The routed spirit flees on dusty heels
    And in the soft fire of a muscatel
Sits up, puts forth its fingertips, and feels—

Down streets so deep the sun can't vault their walls,
Where one-night wives make periodic calls,
 Where cat steals stone where rat makes off with child
And lyre and lute lie down under three balls,

Down blocks in sequence, fact by separate fact,
The human integers add and subtract
 Till in a cubic room in some hotel
You wake one day to find yourself abstract

And turn a knob and hear a voice: *Insist*
On Jiffy Blades, they're tender to the wrist—
 Then static, then a squawk as if your hand
Had shut some human windpipe with a twist.

I know how, lurking under trees by dark,
Poor loony stranglers out to make their mark
 Reach forth shy hands to touch a woman's hair—
I pick up after them in Central Park.

| ALL-KNOWING RABBIT

She chews as if she has it in for grass,
Would swallow earth, envelope all of spring.
Her middle waxes big around with womb
Where fetuses like peas in peapods swing.
She nibbles. Hart Crane's bridge is falling down,
The hangman's knot, the stock quotations slip.
Abominable icemen ply their tongs.
The Russians launch their ermine rocketship.
Akim the jangling mason vaults the air
To plaster up the pockmarks in the moon.
The Alps resituate them in Vermont.
While promenading madboys leap through June
The stoic chops his beet-patch with a hoe.
He hurls up row on purple row of beets.
The mole goes deeper underneath the roots.
There is a sound of silence in the bare streets
But the wise rabbit ponders on her tail
All secrets of tomorrow, of the Nile,
Fluffs clover with one delicate toenail
And munches on, with giaconda smile.

| RONDEAU

Violation on a theme by Charles d'Orléans

The world is taking off her clothes
Of snowdrift, rain and strait-laced freeze
And turns, to show forth by degrees
The bosom of a Rose La Rose.

There's not a bud nor bird, Lord knows,
Can keep still in its balconies.
The world is taking off her clothes
Of snowdrift, rain and strait-laced freeze.

Brook become great from melted snows
Wears a last stitch of ice to tease
And sequined, river's last chemise
Undone in a shudder goes—
The world is taking off her clothes.

CONSPIRATOR MY ROSE

Conspirator my rose,
Green thorn of my plot,
Set your clothes adrift,
Assume wind, scare her hot,

Place dust on your head,
Undo a stiff leaf, shiver,
Let her not suppose
She too may last forever.

LADIES LOOKING FOR LICE

after Rimbaud

When the child's forehead is afire with red
Tortures and he longs for vague white dreams to come,
Two enchantress big sisters steal close to his bed
With tinselly fingers, nails of platinum.

By a casement thrown open they sit the child down
Where blue air bathes stealthily the budded stalk
And in his locks thick with dew and along his crown
Their sorceress hands thin and terrible walk.

He traces the song of their hesitant breath,
Spumed honey that feels forth slow tendrils, the hiss
That now and then breaks it: spit blown through the teeth
And sucked back on the lips, or desire for a kiss.

He hears their black lashes beat through the perfume
Of the quiet and a crackle like static: the slice
Of their fingernails, queens of his indolent gloom,
Passing death sentences on little lice.

Now in him a wine mounts: Laziness,
Sound that can drive mad, a harmonica sigh,
And the child feels in time to each slow caress
Rush and recede endlessly the desire to cry.

LEAVE OF ABSENCE

For an instructor in composition

Now the full pear inclines its shape to fall,
The wind persuasive in the looselimbed trees
Meets with each traverse less and less resistance.
Now twitched loose from your academic bough,
You swirl to earth. They call it leave of absence.

When acorns in staccato downfalls spat in dirt
I hear once more at the novelet of manners
Six times projected, seven times ripped up,
Your hunt-and-peck, your cane with rubber stopper
Testing the solidity of the bottom step,

Again your ballpoint spattering with commas
Drab prose of pretty girls. Who wouldn't throw
After ten years his bottle through his pane
And skim to air on neatly graded wings
Each essay on the nonconformity of Thoreau?

Cars crash through leaves—a sound of shuffled papers
Batters my sleep, routs to the wind my dreams—
Some scrape, others cartwheel with dry twicks of stems
While slow as frost through boughs, moves your veined hand
Scoring with red the looseleaves of the themes.

EPITAPH

Once born, once married, once self-drowned,
I take this wave to be my mound.
A tear, dry reader, will suffice:
Nothing once done would I do twice.

SEANCE

The spirit rapped out on the table:
Only the floor of Hell is stable.

SOLITARY CONFINEMENT

She might have stolen from his arms
Except that there was nothing left
To steal. There was the crucifix
Of silver good enough to hock
But how far could she go on it
And what had he left her to pack
And steal away with and lay down
By someone new in a new town?

And so she put the notion back
And turned her look up where the clock,
Green ghost, swept round its tethered hand
That had made off with many nights
But no more could break from its shelf
Than she could quit this bed where breath
By breath these years he'd nailed her fast
Between two thieves, him and herself.

AT THE GHOSTWRITER'S DEATHBED

for J.B.W.

How many statesmen let you move their lips
    Like creaking shutters while they stood there dazed?
What statues did you dedicate? What ships
    Were launched with winds a little money raised?

Good God go, give our ears a bit of ease.
    Here, take your gibber with you. You've
Graven your tombstone in officialese,
    Get under it. Go moan at one remove.

Incomplete spirit in a house laid waste,
    With thinning hands you tweeze threads in your sheet.
Little to hate is left of you. The priest
    Forgives you, gives you flesh and blood to eat.

At cockcrow, helpless for a turn of phrase,
    A hollow teletype forgets to click.
Stiff is the air you tortured with clichés
    And tongueless stands the body politic.

You sigh between our lines. We can't erase
    Your one historic catchphrase. Worn to death
It walks, a murmur from some public face.
    Christ, did we think we'd boarded up your breath?

WHERE ARE THE SNOWS
OF YESTERYEAR?

Ask a harder question. Here.

Here, if Baedeker we trust,
Alexander the august,

Drinking-songs, their tongue forgot,
Emblems round a shattered pot,

Helen for whom fleets cut foam
Indistinguishable loam,

Dierdre, her combustive hair
Filaments of wavelengthed air,

Heroes struck on Homer's lyre
Strummings of the AP wire,

Sweet-papped wolf, wet nurse of Rome
Paperweight for folks back home,

Wall and rampart of the Moor
Laid flat to the guided tour,

Who by the tomb of Ammon-Ra
Crop their Crackerjack and baa,

Who, short-changed of golden fleece,
Fill out forms for the police.

NUDE DESCENDING A STAIRCASE

Toe upon toe, a snowing flesh,
A gold of lemon, root and rind,
She sifts in sunlight down the stairs
With nothing on. Nor on her mind.

We spy beneath the banister
A constant thresh of thigh on thigh—
Her lips imprint the swinging air
That parts to let her parts go by.

One-woman waterfall, she wears
Her slow descent like a long cape
And pausing, on the final stair
Collects her motions into shape.

ONE A.M. WITH VOICES

Hers: What do you squander night for
          In coupling on a page
          Rimes no man pronounces?—
          Is it love or rage?
          The crouched cat pounces dream-mice,
          True mice play blindman's buff.
          For God's sake give the thing a pitch,
          I've lain cold long enough.

His: Did I write rimes for love, sweet mouse,
         Then I'd have taken instead
         A sheaf of verses to my thighs,
         And rage—that's rape indeed.
         You are the single love I have.
         Be still. A further rime
         Plays cat-and-mouse about my head—
         Just a few minutes. I'm
         A mouser that must hunt awake
         With a green eye that roams
         A shivering candle I must bear
         Where shapes twitch in dark rooms.

Hers: More endless rooms, old creeping tom,
          Than light may overtake.
          When did you ever catch a mouse
          But lean ones, wide awake?

The plump drop to the hunter
Who gropes them out when blind—
How can you keep an eye on
Every mousehole of the mind?
Put cat and light out. You shall have
The warmed side of the bed
That sleep may with a breath blow out
This guttering in your head.